Original title:

Ink-Washed Threads Beneath the Fae Copse

Author: Olivia Oja

ISBN HARDBACK: 978-1-80562-809-5

ISBN PAPERBACK: 978-1-80564-330-2

Echoes of Luminous Wanderers

In moonlit groves where shadows sigh,
The wanderers dance, their spirits high.
With flickering lights, they guide the way,
Through whispered dreams that drift and sway.

Echoes of laughter float on the breeze,
Like silver threads woven through the trees.
Each step a story, a tale untold,
Of ancient paths where magic unfolds.

Stars above twinkle with knowing grace,
As wanderers tread through time and space.
Their journey marked by stardust bright,
Illuminating the depths of night.

With every heartbeat, they chase the dawn,
By crystal streams where the night is drawn.
Luminous spirits of forgotten lore,
Forever seeking, forever more.

In the silence, a promise remains,
That wanderers find the truth in chains.
With echoes soft, they'll pave the route,
For those who follow, without a doubt.

The Tapestry of Whispered Sorrows

Threads of twilight paint the sky,
As shadows linger, and spirits sigh.
In woven tales of love and pain,
The tapestry glimmers, soft yet plain.

Each thread a story, lost but found,
In hidden corners of the town.
Where whispered sorrows meet the light,
And guide the heart, through endless night.

In every heart, a tapestry spun,
With colors of battles lost and won.
The pain of longing, the joy of grace,
Each stitch a memory we cannot erase.

Yet through the sorrow, hope takes flight,
Transforming darkness into light.
As we unravel the tangled seam,
We find the strength in each shared dream.

A fragile heart can heal anew,
With threads of friendship, strong and true.
In the quiet hush, let love bestow,
A tapestry rich with what we know.

Beneath Shimmering Canopies of Wonder

Beneath the leaves, where secrets dwell,
A world of magic begins to swell.
With laughter ringing through the trees,
And dancing light on gentle breeze.

Wonders blossom in hidden nooks,
Where streams are filled with tales from books.
Beneath the canopies, dreams take flight,
In the sweetest embrace of softening light.

Colors swirl in the twilight glow,
As daisies whisper to the crow.
A symphony plays, both wild and sweet,
In nature's arms, our hearts will meet.

With every step, the forest sings,
With stories woven on fairy wings.
Among the roots, where the wild things play,
We learn to see in a wondrous way.

So close your eyes and breathe it in,
Let the magic in your heart begin.
For beneath these canopies of wonder,
The world is waiting, pure as thunder.

The Cartographer's Heart in Woodland Realms

In woodland realms where silence reigns,
The cartographer maps the secret lanes.
With ink and dreams beneath the stars,
He charts the echoes of ancient wars.

Each compass point a whispered plea,
With every line, a memory.
Of moonlit paths and twilight's spark,
In quiet woods where shadows hark.

His heart is filled with tales untold,
Of distant lands and treasures bold.
With parchment worn from years of quest,
He carries legends in his chest.

Through tangled roots and gnarled trees,
He seeks the truth upon the breeze.
With every journey, hope expands,
Unfolding magic across the lands.

And when the dawn begins to break,
He turns to chart another wake.
For in his heart, the world will blend,
The cartographer's journey will never end.

Dreams Stitched in Emerald Shadows

Beneath the boughs of ancient trees,
A whispered tale adrift in breeze.
Where moonlight weaves through emerald seams,
And dances gently with our dreams.

In shadows deep, where secrets lie,
A silver mist begins to sigh.
The nightingale sings soft and low,
As starlight paints the world aglow.

Each petal glimmers, draped in Night,
With threads of hope, a wondrous sight.
Through tangled roots, our fancies tread,
In this twilight realm, where all is said.

The echoes of the past arise,
In every glitter, truth belies.
We chase the whispers, light and free,
In dreams stitched tight by destiny.

Awake we'll be, when dawn draws near,
Yet in our hearts, the night is clear.
For every shadow that we chase,
Holds a stitch of our laced grace.

Enigma of the Faerie Glade

In twilight's hue, the faeries prance,
With laughter sweet, and woven dance.
Their wings like petals, soft and light,
Reveal the secrets of the night.

A glade adorned with petals rare,
Where fireflies weave the evening air.
Each flicker tells a tale untold,
Of ancient magics bright and bold.

A shimmering brook hums tunes of old,
Reflecting dreams and wishes bold.
Amongst the trees, the whispers play,
An enigma carved in night and day.

With every step, a story grows,
In this enchanted world that glows.
The air is thick with dreams to share,
In the faerie glade, beyond compare.

Yet shadows linger just outside,
A gentle warning, foreign tide.
For every joy, a price it seems,
In the enigma of our dreams.

Celestial Strokes on Timid Blades

Upon the hill where wisps do trace,
The strokes of stars in velvet space.
With timid blades of emerald grass,
Where dreams unfold and moments pass.

A nightingale croons from shyly high,
Its melody a soft, sweet sigh.
Each note a brush, each chord a light,
Painting wishes in the night.

Celestial winks through velvet shades,
Scattered glow, where silence wades.
With every breath, the cosmos hums,
A lullaby as starlight strums.

We lay beneath the tender sky,
In gentle peace where hopes can fly.
For in this realm of soft embrace,
Celestial strokes weave time and space.

With every whisper softly spun,
A tapestry of dreams begun.
And in this quiet, hearts may find,
The strokes of stars, forever kind.

Veils of Twilight Over Fauna's Dance

Between the trees where shadows sigh,
A dance unfolds beneath the sky.
With veils of twilight woven fine,
The creatures sway to rhythms divine.

The fox with grace, the owl with flair,
In gentle harmony, they share.
The moonlight spills like silver wine,
A symphony in every line.

Beneath the boughs, the whispers crawl,
A secret pulsing through it all.
In twilight's charm, the wild things prance,
Awash in joy, they seize the chance.

Each flicker of a firefly bright,
Marks the cadence of the night.
With every leap, they lose their woes,
In dances bright where magic flows.

Yet as the night begins to wane,
With softest sighs, they know the gain.
For in their hearts, they'll hold the trance,
Of veils of twilight over their dance.

Interwoven Paths of Faery Grace

Through whispering woods, where shadows play,
Twinkling lights lead the lost astray.
Elfin laughter fills the chill,
Guiding hearts with a gentle thrill.

Beneath the boughs, where secrets dwell,
Stories of old, the faeries tell.
With each soft step, the world unfolds,
A tapestry of dreams in golds.

Moonbeams dance on a silver brook,
Unraveled tales in every nook.
Spinning joy in the dusky haze,
Embraced by night's enchanting gaze.

Time stands still in this hallowed space,
Magic lingers, a tender grace.
Through interwoven paths we roam,
A journey shared, forever home.

As dawn breaks, the faeries hide,
Yet in our hearts, they will abide.
In every laugh, in every sigh,
Their spirit sings, an endless high.

The Elixir of Twilight Shadows

In the twilight's soft embrace,
Dreams unfold in whispered grace.
A potion brewed from dusk's own tears,
Awakens hope, dispels our fears.

Shadows dance beneath the boughs,
Eldritch whispers forge our vows.
The elixir glows with twilight's hue,
Reviving hearts worn out and blue.

With every drop, the world renews,
A tapestry of vibrant views.
Crafting wonder in the night,
As starlit skies ignite delight.

Lost in the spell of gentle night,
We wander where the dreamers write.
Each moment sipped, a cherished thrill,
The elixir warms, our spirits fill.

As dawn peeks through the shadowed veil,
We carry forth the twilight tale.
In every heart, a memory stays,
The magic lingers, softly plays.

Fables Woven in Foliate Dreams

In the embrace of leafy glades,
Fables spin in nature's shades.
Whispers twist like ivy's climb,
Growing rich with breaths of time.

Each leaf tells stories of the past,
Of lovers lost and spells cast.
Crafted dreams in emerald hue,
Where sunlight breaks, the shadows too.

Time may fray this fragile thread,
Yet in its weave, new hopes are bred.
Tender tales of heart's desires,
Ignite the mind with kindled fires.

Beneath the boughs, we find our place,
In the fable of all time's grace.
Woven tight, our dreams take flight,
Bound by love, embraced by light.

As seasons change, the stories grow,
In every heartbeat, they overflow.
Each foliate dream, a cherished seam,
In the tapestry of life's great dream.

Echoes of Laughter Beneath Canopy Gold

In the glade where sunlight spills,
Laughter echoes, the heart it fills.
Children of the earth unite,
Beneath the canopy of light.

Golden leaves drift soft and slow,
Carrying joy from the hearts below.
A symphony of playful grace,
We dance through time, a bright embrace.

With every giggle, the world ignites,
Transforming days into cherished nights.
In every moment, the magic grows,
As wonder blooms like a fragrant rose.

Through rustling trees, the laughter flows,
Weaving tales only nature knows.
In this realm, all fears take flight,
Embraced in joy, we chase the light.

As shadows stretch, our spirits soar,
In laughter's echo, we long for more.
Together, we weave a tapestry bold,
Of memories bright, beneath canopy gold.

Chasing Fireflies Through Forgotten Dells

In twilight's grasp, we danced and spun,
With laughter light as the evening sun.
Each flicker glimmers, the night alive,
In secret glades where the dreams arrive.

We wove through woods, where shadows play,
Where whispers tell of the end of day.
The fireflies flit, like stars set free,
Lighting the path where our hearts can be.

The scent of grass, the cool night's breath,
In tender moments, we flirt with death.
With every spark, a wish unfolds,
In the soft embrace of dusk so bold.

We chase the trails of golden lights,
In harmony with our heart's delights.
Forgotten dells, where magic stirs,
A world enchanted, where nothing blurs.

In night's sweet serenade, we find,
The threads of wonder knit intertwined.
Through fireflies' chorus, our spirits soar,
In timeless realms, forevermore.

Fragments of Time in the Boughs Above

Up in the branches, secrets lay,
Time's gentle whispers, they drift and sway.
Each rustling leaf a memory spun,
Of countless ages, lost and won.

The wind carries tales from days of yore,
As shadows cast on the forest floor.
Fragments of time, in the sun's warm glow,
In every bough, where the wild hearts go.

With beams of light, they softly prance,
Inviting dreams in a fleeting dance.
We listen close, as the echoes weave,
A tapestry bright, for those who believe.

In golden glimmers, the past reborn,
Each moment cherished, each moment worn.
The boughs above, they cradle the night,
Holding our wishes, keeping them bright.

As night descends, the stars take flight,
In sylvan halls where shadows ignite.
Fragments of time, they shimmer and twine,
In every heartbeat, forever align.

Light and Shadow in Faery Whispers

In hidden groves where secrets dwell,
The faeries sing their enchanting spell.
Light and shadow dance on the ground,
With every note, new magic found.

Gentle breezes carry soft sighs,
From creatures born under velvet skies.
They flit and flutter, with laughter sweet,
In the silent realms where dreamers meet.

The glimmer of stardust on twilight's face,
Brings forth a wild and wondrous grace.
In murmurs soft, they weave their lore,
Through night's embrace, forevermore.

With every heartbeat, shadows drift,
As faery whispers create a rift.
Between the worlds, they twine and tease,
In fragrant meadows kissed by the breeze.

So heed the call of the hidden glen,
Where light and shadow unite again.
In faery whispers, our souls take flight,
Guided by stars through the velvet night.

Celestial Secrets in the Underbrush

Beneath the leaves, where silence reigns,
Celestial secrets in twilight's veins.
Among the roots, the stories flow,
Of worlds unseen, where spirits glow.

In dampened earth, a soft embrace,
Whispers arise from a hidden place.
The underbrush cradles ancient dreams,
Where life unfurls in gentle streams.

Each fluttering moth, each creeping vine,
Carries the weight of the divine.
In moonlit shadows, the truth is spun,
A tapestry woven by stars undone.

We wander lost in the fragrant night,
Where wild things wander and hearts take flight.
Celestial secrets, brave and bright,
In the tangled paths, we find our light.

Amongst the whispers, we seek the key,
Unlocking the tales that dare to be.
In the underbrush, beneath the sky,
Celestial wonders softly lie.

Camouflaged Memories Under Lacy Boughs

In whispers soft as twilight's hush,
The old trees sway with secrets' rush.
Beneath the lacy boughs they weave,
A tapestry of hearts that cleave.

Time's gentle hand has brushed the leaves,
Where laughter flows, and sorrow grieves.
The fleeting shadows dance and play,
On memories that will not stray.

Each dappled light of golden hue,
Holds stories that the winds once knew.
In every creak and swaying limb,
Echoes of love that never dim.

Underneath the boughs, the past resides,
In cradled dreams where hope abides.
Yet, with each rustle, whispers reign,
Of moments lost, and lingering pain.

Feel the breeze, let it take flight,
Through all the shades of day and night.
For in this grove, we find our truth,
Camouflaged memories of our youth.

A Glimpse of Gossamer Realms

In twilight's breath, a shimmer glows,
Through veils of mist, a secret flows.
Fairies weave their silent threads,
In dreams where gentle magic spreads.

A glimpse of realms where wonders play,
In gossamer dreams, we drift away.
With moonlit trails that beckon near,
Whispers of joy, devoid of fear.

Stars twinkle bright, a guiding hand,
Leading seekers to that distant land.
With every step on starlit paths,
We dance through echoes of soft laughs.

Each flicker bright, each tender sound,
In timeless realms where love is found.
A world that thrives beyond the veil,
Where hopes and dreams begin to sail.

Dive deep into that lumined sea,
Where laughter flows eternally free.
In this embrace, where spirits soar,
A gossamer realm forevermore.

Murmurs of the Heart Beneath Ancient Trees

Beneath the canopy, shadows hum,
As ancient trees in silence drum.
Whispers weave through leafy green,
In nature's heart, we find the unseen.

Murmurs rise with the evening light,
Echoing dreams that take to flight.
Branches sway in a gentle dance,
Inviting the heart to take its chance.

Roots embrace the soil's deep lore,
History's pulse beats at the core.
Every leaf a story told,
Of battles fought, and love grown old.

The heart's soft thrum, a steady beat,
As time unveils the treasured seat.
In quiet moments, secrets share,
Beneath the trees, our burdens bare.

Let us listen to nature's song,
Where every heartbeat feels so strong.
In this haven where we convene,
Murmurs of love, forever green.

Petals and Phantoms in Dusk's Embrace

In dusky light, where shadows play,
Petals fall in a soft ballet.
A whisper of night in fragrant bloom,
As phantoms gather in the gloom.

The twilight hums a haunting tune,
In a garden kissed by the moon.
Colors blend in a fading light,
Where dreams float softly into night.

Each petal tells a story old,
Of love and loss, of hearts so bold.
In every sigh, the night reveals,
The magic that this stillness heals.

Through tangled vines, the secrets grow,
In shadows deep, where no one knows.
Yet in this dusk, a warmth entwines,
Binding all in tender lines.

So linger here, with me a while,
In dusk's embrace, let hearts compile.
For in this realm of petals' grace,
Phantoms dance in a timeless space.

A Palette of Ethereal Dreams

In twilight realms where shadows play,
A canvas blooms, both night and day.
Whispers of colors, soft and bright,
Dance in the corners of fading light.

Brush of a star, with glimmers rare,
Sketches of hopes entwined with air.
Each stroke a tale of hearts in flight,
A symphony sung in silent night.

Beneath the moon, where wishes glow,
A spectrum spells the paths we know.
In dreams we weave, with gentle hands,
A tapestry of distant lands.

With every hue, a secret shared,
In every sigh, a soul laid bare.
The ethereal whispers call us near,
In painted realms, we face our fear.

As dawn unfolds, the colors bleed,
In silent woods, where hearts take heed.
Each palette shift, a life anew,
In every dream, the world breaks through.

Mosaic of Fractured Starlight

Beneath the sky of shattered glass,
Where echoes linger, moments pass.
A mosaic formed by time's own hand,
In pieces scattered across the land.

Each fragment tells a tale of old,
In shimmering hues, brave and bold.
Caught in the weave of night's embrace,
A cosmic dance, an endless chase.

Whispers of light through darkness seep,
Awakening dreams from timeless sleep.
Stars that flicker, dim, then gleam,
In patterns woven like a dream.

Fragments twirl in the vast expanse,
While lovers find their fated dance.
With every pulse, a story spun,
In twilight's glow, two hearts are one.

The canvas shifts, the tale grows bright,
In laughter shared and pure delight.
A mosaic of our whispered fates,
Where hopes are stitched through ornate gates.

Threads of Silence in the Dappled Shade

In dappled light, where secrets rest,
Threads of silence weave their quest.
A gentle breeze wraps branches low,
Weaving whispers where shadows grow.

Fluttering leaves in softest sighs,
Catch the lull of the morning skies.
Each moment cherished, delicate thread,
Binds the heart with words unsaid.

Beneath the boughs where dreams take flight,
The world is hushed, bathed in light.
Rambling thoughts and laughter stray,
In dappled shade where children play.

Gossamer strands of golden sun,
Embrace the earth, where roots run.
In stillness found, a joyous hum,
Unraveled tales, where voices come.

The moments linger, sweet and clear,
In nature's arms, we draw near.
Threads of silence, a gentle balm,
In the dappled shade, the heart finds calm.

The Magic of Sunlit Palette

Upon the hills where daisies sway,
A sunlit palette starts the day.
Colors burst with laughter and grace,
In the light, the world finds its place.

Golden strokes in the morning dew,
Paint the sky in every hue.
Nature's brush, with a careful hand,
Crafts a story across the land.

Each petal holds a whisper sweet,
In every corner, life's heartbeat.
With warmth that wraps like a tender hug,
The magic dances, a joyful tug.

Beneath the beams where shadows rest,
The tapestry spins, alive and blessed.
Flowing rivers and gentle streams,
Keep the palette of our dreams.

As twilight comes, the colors fade,
Yet in our hearts, the memories wade.
The magic holds, in every breath,
A sunlit palette, where love bequeaths.

The Allure of Forgotten Sylvan Stories

In forests deep where shadows lie,
Whispers of tales both low and high,
The ancient trees keep secrets close,
Of magic lost and promises rose.

A flicker of light on a mossy stone,
Reminds us we're never truly alone,
For in the rustle of leaves we hear,
The laughter of sprites, so sweet and clear.

A brook sings soft, a melody old,
Of heroes brave and treasures told,
In every ripple, the stories flow,
Of battles fought for love's warm glow.

With every step upon this ground,
New wonders wait, waiting to be found,
For those who dare to heed the call,
Will find the magic wrapped in thrall.

So linger now, let your heart roam free,
In meadow's dance, 'neath the grand old trees,
For in the silence, the magic wakes,
And sprightly fables twine like snakes.

Veils of Twilight Wrapped in Scenic Enigma

Twilight drapes the world in grace,
An ethereal hush in time and space,
The moon peeks through in silver guise,
Inviting dreams beneath starlit skies.

Winds carry scents of mystery vast,
Hints of the future, echoes of the past,
In shadows thick where visions blend,
Life's tapestry weaves, a tale without end.

Each moment glows with secrets untold,
As twilight softens the edges bold,
The realm between what's false and real,
Holds wonders waiting for hearts to feel.

In every corner, a story waits,
Wrapped in the tendrils of fate's own gates,
With each heartbeat, the night comes alive,
In the dance of darkness, dreams shall arrive.

So breathe and listen, let visions rise,
In the twilight's embrace, where magic lies,
Each whispering shadow, a soft refrain,
Unfolding the mystery, the joy, the pain.

Visions of the Wild on Wistful Winds

Along the path where the wild things roam,
Nature's whispers feel like home,
Sunlight dapples through branches wide,
As the heart beats strong, untried, untried.

The call of the wild dances in the air,
A symphony crafted with utmost care,
Every breeze a gentle sigh,
Of spirits free, they soar and fly.

The rustle of wings, a fleeting glance,
In vibrant meadows, all creatures prance,
With every pulse of the earth's own song,
You find a place where you belong.

Let the wild winds guide your feet,
In every corner, adventure meets,
For in the whispers of roots and leaves,
The wild beckons, the heart believes.

So let your spirit stretch and twine,
With nature's pulse, where dreams entwine,
For visions of wonder on winds so pure,
Will lead you forth to the great allure.

Blurred Realities Beneath the Whispering Boughs

Beneath the boughs where shadows play,
Reality blurs, night swallows day,
Mirrored thoughts flicker in the light,
As dreams weave through the soft of night.

The forest breathes, a living dream,
With echoes of laughter, a mystical theme,
Where echoes and whispers embrace the stars,
Creating a dance that heals the scars.

In twilight's grip, the senses awake,
To spectres of stories the night will make,
In the dance of the fireflies lost and found,
Where the rhythm of magic knows no bound.

With every rustle, a tale's rebirth,
Of hidden treasures, of love and mirth,
So linger low, let magic in,
The stories of yore are yours to spin.

For in the hush where time stands still,
Life intertwines with the ancient will,
Beneath the boughs where shadows play,
The world transforms in wondrous ways.

Whispers of the Sylvan Stream

In the heart of the woods, where the soft waters glide,
Nature hums softly, as the trees gently bide.
Moss carpets the bank, a lush emerald throne,
Where secrets of time in each ripple are sown.

The silver fish dart, in a synchronized dance,
Caught in the spell of the stream's gentle trance.
Murmurs of magic twine in the air,
A symphony woven with tenderest care.

Sunlight dappled through leaves, a flickering muse,
Invites dreams to wander, as one cannot refuse.
The breeze brings a story from far and from near,
Whispers of creatures who thrived without fear.

Creeping ivy clings to the ancient oak's frame,
While shadows grow longer, yet never the same.
Time softly lingers, as moments unfold,
A tapestry rich with the colors of gold.

Where the sylvan stream flows, hearts come to renew,
In the hush of the forest, beneath skies of blue.
Life dances in echoes, a mystical theme,
Forever alive in the whispers of stream.

Shadows Cast by Moonlit Canopy

In the silence of night, when the stars softly gleam,
Shadows stretch long, weaving dark with a dream.
Moonlight bathes all in a silvery glow,
Painting the forest, where wild spirits flow.

Branches entwined like the fingers of fate,
Guard ancient secrets, they silently sate.
Beneath this broad arch, the world basks in peace,
As enchantments abound, and all sorrows cease.

Nightjars sing softly, a lullaby rare,
Embracing the shadows that drift in the air.
Through whispers of pines, the cool breezes sigh,
Filling the darkness with echoes of why.

The owls turn their gaze, wise sentinels high,
Watching the woodlands, they silently pry.
Each rustle, each flutter, a tale to be told,
Of courage and wonder, of laughter and bold.

In moonlit embrace, where all spirits converge,
The night holds its breath, in a celestial surge.
For here under stars, in the shadows they meet,
The stories of old in retreat and repeat.

Elven Secrets in Twilight Glades

In glades where the twilight weaves fabric so fine,
The elegance dances on petals divine.
Elven folk gather, with laughter so light,
Sharing their secrets in the hush of the night.

Glimmers of starlight spark joy in their eyes,
As shadows weave tales 'neath the vast velvet skies.
Whispers of harmony echo the breeze,
Soft notes intertwine with the rustling of leaves.

With feet bare on earth, they twirl 'round the boughs,
In reverence of life, amidst beauty's vows.
Cherished traditions, from ages gone past,
In twilight's embrace, their allure holds fast.

The moon weaves a tapestry, silver and bright,
Illuminating hearts that take flight in the night.
Each story a gem in the crown of the wood,
A chorus of dreams where the magic once stood.

In these sacred glades, where the day softly fades,
Elven secrets linger in the soft, leafy shades.
A dance of the timeless, so rich and so grand,
In the twilight's soft arms, they forever shall stand.

Ephemeral Designs on Gossamer Wings

In the hush of dawn, when the world starts to wake,
Gossamer wings flutter, no burden, no ache.
Delicate patterns, like lace in the air,
Dance to the rhythm of dreams, bold and rare.

Each insect a painter, with hues soft and bright,
Creating a canvas of splendor and light.
Ephemeral whispers float high on the breeze,
A moment, a vision, to seize with great ease.

They flit through the gardens, in sunlit embrace,
Each one a small marvel, each flight a new grace.
They shimmer like jewels, in the soft morning glow,
Breaking the silence where wildflowers grow.

As day melts to twilight, their brilliance will fade,
Yet the memory lingers in colors arrayed.
For beauty is fleeting, like dew on the grass,
A moment, a glimpse—a sweet sigh as they pass.

Celebrate those designs as they dance in the light,
Carrying whispers of joy in their flight.
For in every flutter, a story is spun,
On gossamer wings, where all life is begun.

Luminous Trails Through the Sylphic Glade

In whispers soft, the moonlight glows,
Through sylphic glades where magic flows.
The twinkling stars above align,
As secrets dance in woodlands fine.

Among the trees, the shadows play,
With every step, the fairies sway.
Their laughter sparkles through the air,
A melody, both sweet and rare.

The brook sings tales of ages past,
Of dreams that linger, shadows cast.
Each glimmering trail, a path revealed,
In nature's heart, the truth concealed.

Oh, follow where the willows weep,
Into the depths where whispers seep.
The night's embrace, so soft and kind,
In sylphic glades, our hearts entwined.

As dawn awakes, the colors bloom,
In golden rays, dispelling gloom.
Yet in the morn, the magic stays,
In luminous trails, a trace of ways.

Pensive Whispers Among the Glimmering Ferns

In quiet nooks, the ferns reside,
With gentle grace, they softly glide.
A pensive breeze, a lover's sigh,
Awakens thoughts, where memories lie.

The glimmering dew, like pearls displayed,
Each droplet holds a story made.
Beneath the boughs, the whispers tread,
Of dreams deferred and words unsaid.

A tale unfolds in leafy hues,
Of laughter shared and tender views.
The forest listens, wise and old,
To secrets spun in earth's soft fold.

The shadows weave through sunlit glen,
In tales of yore, we meet again.
With every rustle, thoughts ignite,
In pensive whispers, day turns to night.

And as the twilight starts to glow,
The ferns embrace the ebb and flow.
In every moment, pure and true,
Their glimmering grace feels fresh as dew.

The Language of Leaves in Dreamlike Flutters

In whispered tones the leaves unfold,
A language lost, in tales retold.
With dreamlike flutters, they convey,
The stories held in sun's warm sway.

A gentle rustle, a soft refrain,
Brings forth a sigh of joy and pain.
They tell of breezes, secrets rife,
Of distant worlds and blooming life.

Each leaf a word, a verse composed,
In nature's breath, their beauty glows.
In shades of green, their message clear,
An ancient song for all to hear.

In autumn's fire, their colors sing,
A symphony of change they bring.
Like whispers shared 'neath twilight skies,
The language speaks where silence lies.

So let us listen, hearts attuned,
To whispered tales by nature crooned.
In dreamlike flutters, truth unfolds,
The language of leaves, forever holds.

Sketches of Light in Nature's Vein

In golden hues the sunlight plays,
Sketching dreams in soft arrays.
Through leaves and blooms, it weaves a thread,
Of vibrant tales and words unsaid.

Each beam a brush, the world a canvas,
Where shadows dance, and moments amass.
A flutter here, a sparkle there,
In nature's vein, the art laid bare.

The gentle stream reflects the sky,
A symphony of colors high.
With every ripple, magic flows,
In sketches formed where beauty grows.

As dusk approaches, hues entwine,
The fading light, a rare design.
In every twilight's tender glow,
Nature's art begins to show.

So let us wander, eyes aglow,
In sketches bright where wonders flow.
For in this realm, all hearts can gain,
The gift of light in nature's vein.

Mysteries Entwined in Dew-Kissed Leaves

In the hush of dawn's embrace,
Whispers float on gentle breeze,
Secrets woven in the lace,
Nature sighs beneath the trees.

Dewdrops glisten, soft and bright,
Truths concealed in emerald folds,
Morning's magic, pure delight,
Each leaf tells what time beholds.

Beneath the elder's watchful gaze,
Twilight dances with the day,
Lost in nature's wondrous maze,
Mysteries in shadows play.

Quiet footsteps tread the ground,
Echoes of a past long gone,
In the silence, truths are found,
Through the leaves, the light has shone.

Entwined like fate in threads of green,
Wonders beckon, soft and low,
In each fiber, sights unseen,
Dew-kissed whispers, stories flow.

Faery Tales Etched in Nature's Canvas

In glades where magic stirs the air,
Tiny dreams on willows swing,
Painted blooms in colors rare,
Nature's brush begins to sing.

Mushroom circles twirl with glee,
Underneath the ancient oaks,
Faery laughter, wild and free,
Nature's breath in whispered jokes.

Crickets chirp a midnight tune,
While the stars compose a dance,
Fleeting shadows chase the moon,
In this realm, we take our chance.

Petals shimmer, stories told,
By the brook's soft, flowing hand,
Each leaf a voice, a heart of gold,
In this enchanted, timeless land.

Every glimmer, every hue,
Carries tales of love and strife,
Etched in nature, pure and true,
Faery magic, breath of life.

Starlit Ribbons of Forgotten Lore

Underneath the midnight sky,
Whispers weave through shadows deep,
Ancient stories drift and sigh,
In the silence, secrets keep.

Stars like dancers, soft and bright,
Spin their tales in threads of gold,
Starlit paths in velvet night,
Guiding hearts to truths untold.

Galaxies, they hum and swell,
Drawing dreams from long ago,
In their light, the spirits dwell,
Magic flows like rivers slow.

Tales of wanderers and kings,
Caught in starlight's sacred blend,
Each a gift that time still brings,
As the night begins to mend.

Ribbons stretch across the sky,
Binding past with present's pulse,
In their glow, we learn to fly,
Chasing echoes, soft and dulled.

Ephemeral Colors of Nature's Heart

In the garden where dreams bloom,
Colors blend, a fleeting grace,
Sunlight spills, dispels the gloom,
Nature's touch, a warm embrace.

Crimson petals, hues of dawn,
Butterflies in soft ballet,
With each heartbeat, blooms are gone,
Ephemeral, they fade away.

Morning glories peek and smile,
Waltzing with the gentle breeze,
In their beauty, rest awhile,
Nature's brush brings hearts to ease.

Golden leaves like whispers fall,
Painting paths of whispered tales,
In this fleeting, wondrous call,
Life unfurls as each heart fails.

Colors pure, a canvas bright,
In their warmth, we come alive,
Ephemeral shades ignite,
Nature's heart forever thrives.

Whispers of the Enchanted Grove

In the heart of the woods where magic stirs,
Whispers weave through the leaves, softly purrs.
Old oaks stand guard, their branches held high,
Cradling secrets as days drift by.

Beneath the glow of twilight's soft kiss,
Creatures emerge from the shadows of bliss.
A rustle, a flutter, the wind finds its voice,
In this realm of wonder, the heart has no choice.

Moss blankets the earth, a comforting shroud,
While fireflies dance in a luminous crowd.
Every sigh of the forest tells tales untold,
Of kingdoms forgotten, of heroes bold.

With every step taken on this ancient path,
The spirits awaken, igniting their wrath.
Yet laughter lingers in the glades so deep,
A song of enchantment that lulls one to sleep.

On gnarled branches, a soft melody strums,
The rhythm of life as the evening hums.
In the whispers of trees, their secrets unfold,
The magic of the grove, a treasure of old.

Shadows Dance in Gossamer Light

With each rising moon, shadows softly arise,
In gossamer light, where enchantment lies.
A waltz of the night, where the echoes play,
As the stars whisper magic, guiding the way.

Veils of mist drape o'er the silvery ground,
While unseen spirits gather around.
With whispers of secrets and songs of the past,
They beckon the dreamers, their fates intertwined fast.

In the depths of the night, where time seems to freeze,
The wind carries stories, dancing through trees.
Every flicker of light, a reminder of hope,
In shadows that flicker, our spirits elope.

A tapestry woven of night's gentle grace,
Where moonlight and shadows together embrace.
The laughter of fairies, a harmonious tune,
As the world spins in wonder beneath silvered moon.

As dawn tips her hat, the shadows recede,
Yet the magic endures, forever to lead.
In the heart of the night, an adventure begins,
For those who seek wonders, where the true journey spins.

Secrets Woven in Moonlit Mist

In the still of the night, when the world holds its breath,
Moonlit mist drapes softly, a whisper of death.
Secrets lay hidden in the shimmer so pale,
Where shadows retreat and the dreams set sail.

Beneath the soft glow of the delicate skies,
Where echoes of laughter mask low, grieving sighs.
A path lined with wonders, blossoms in bloom,
In the embrace of the night, there's no room for gloom.

Glowing orbs chase the darkness away,
As the chorus of crickets leads the ballet.
Down winding trails, through the enchanted air,
The moon weaves her magic, a dance we all share.

Soft whispers of starlight entwine with the breeze,
Telling tales of enchantment that sway through the trees.
On the wings of the night, old stories take flight,
As secrets emerge, woven in moonlit light.

So, linger a moment, embrace this delight,
For the world feels alive in this mystical night.
Where magic lies waiting, just beyond sight,
In the mysteries cloaked by the moon's gentle light.

Fluttering Ephemera of the Sylvan Realm

Among ancient trees, where the shadows play,
Ephemeral flutterings drift through the day.
Tiny wings whisper in sunlight's embrace,
As the sylvan realm dances, a delicate grace.

A tapestry woven of colors so bright,
In meadows ablaze with the warmth of the light.
With laughter and joy, the wildflowers sway,
As fluttering creatures explore their own way.

From dew-kissed petals, a sweet fragrance gleams,
In the heart of the forest, where reality dreams.
Every breeze carries chuckles from high,
As echoes of laughter float up to the sky.

In this sylvan haven, where time drifts afar,
The magic lies hidden in each twinkling star.
With every soft flutter, a wish takes its flight,
In the whispers of nature, our spirits alight.

So wander through realms where the faeries still dwell,
In the heart of the woods, where enchantments compel.
For in every moment, in this world so surreal,
Lie fluttering ephemera, the magic we feel.

Secrets Hidden in the Fern's Stalk

In shadows deep, where secrets dwell,
The fern's soft fronds weave tales to tell.
Whispers of magic lost in the green,
Guardians of mysteries yet unseen.

Beneath the leaves, the old roots twist,
Each silent promise, an ancient tryst.
Time weaves a spell, a silken thread,
Among the ferns where dreams are led.

A glimmer awaits in the morning's dew,
A fleeting glimpse of the wonders true.
The nutty scent of earth and moss,
Cloaks the treasure, heavy as a cross.

Listen close, to the rustling sighs,
Where the heart of nature gently lies.
In every curl, a secret rests,
Within the fern, the past tests.

So wander forth, with eyes wide bright,
Seek the wonders hidden from sight.
For in the stillness, the soul can learn,
The lasting lore, the fern's return.

Threads of Destiny Woven in Dappled Shade

In the dappled light where shadows play,
The threads of fate glide in ballet.
Each step we take, a choice to make,
In the forest's heart, the dreams we stake.

Nature's loom spins stories fine,
In every rustle, a spark divine.
With whispers sweet, the branches sway,
Binding all lives in a tapestry's way.

Underneath the boughs where spirits tread,
A path unfolds where few have led.
The twist of time in every breeze,
Weaving connections among the trees.

The dance of fate, a fragile song,
In this enchanted place, we all belong.
With every heartbeat, a thread we weave,
In dappled shade, we learn to believe.

So heed the murmurs, take your chance,
Join the dance in the forest's expanse.
For in this realm of shadow and light,
Our destinies twist, both day and night.

Enigmas of the Night-Blooming Flora

When dusk unfurls its velvet sheets,
The night-blooming flowers bring forth their feats.
In fragrant whispers, they weave the dark,
Telling secrets in night's soft spark.

Petals awaken with the moon's soft glow,
An ode to beauty that few may know.
Beneath the stars, they open wide,
Unraveling tales they choose to hide.

In shadows deep, where mysteries twine,
The flora unfolds, enigmatic and fine.
With silver dew as their gentle cloak,
They share their lore, softly spoke.

The still of the night, the rustle of leaves,
Hold the secrets that nature weaves.
For each bloom holds both joy and strife,
In the dance of the shadows, the cycle of life.

So wander through gardens where night blooms thrive,
And let their magic help you survive.
For in the quiet, the heart can hear,
The enigmas spoken, crystal clear.

The Liquid Silence of Woodland Whispers

In the woodland's heart, a silence flows,
Like liquid shadows, where nobody goes.
Each rustle low, each crackle slight,
Holds a secret of day and night.

The trees stand tall, guardians of lore,
With branches that reach for stories of yore.
In the hush of dusk, a soft voice sings,
Echoing the wisdom that silence brings.

Footfalls soft on the carpeted ground,
Each whispered breath, a solace found.
The air, a tapestry, woven so fine,
Wraps us in calm, a touch divine.

The brook that babbles in jovial cheer,
Knows the confessions of all who come near.
And in the twilight, the secrets blend,
In liquid silence, the woods transcend.

So linger awhile, in this sacred space,
Let the stillness wrap you in its embrace.
For in the woodland whispers, we find,
The truths of our heart, intertwined.

Traces of Dreams in Leafy Halls

In leafy halls where whispers dwell,
Faint echoing dreams weave stories to tell.
Moonlit shadows dance on trees,
As secrets drift upon the breeze.

Ferns and ivy cloak the past,
Memories linger, shadows cast.
In silence, each leaf a page,
Unfolding tales of joy and rage.

Branches arch in knowing grace,
Cradling moments in this space.
Twinkling stars the night adorn,
As dreams in leafy halls are born.

From twilight's edge to dawn's embrace,
A symphony of time and place.
In gentle rustles, hope aligns,
In the heart of nature, truth entwines.

So tread softly on the ground,
Where ancient echoes can be found.
For in these halls, where dreams do roam,
One finds in leaves their quiet home.

Dances of Light in Enchanted Groves

In enchanted groves where light cascades,
Sunbeams weave through the verdant blades.
A ballet of shadows, they twirl and spin,
As laughter and joy play soft within.

Whispers of fairies brush the air,
As petals tremble, light and fair.
Crickets serenade the blissful night,
In this realm of magic, pure delight.

Beneath the boughs, where secrets lie,
Each flickering sparkle tells a sigh.
With every step, the wonder grows,
As twilight deepens, the moonlight glows.

A tapestry of dreams unfolds,
In this grove, where warmth enfolds.
Hearts entwined in the dance of fate,
Embracing the magic, never late.

So let the light guide your way,
In enchanted groves where shadows play.
Dance with the spirits, join the song,
In harmony, you will belong.

The Veil Between Worlds in Silken Hues

In silken hues where worlds collide,
A fabric spun where dreams confide.
Between the strands of dusk and dawn,
The veil invites the weary on.

Softly woven, the whispers call,
In twilight's glow, we stand enthralled.
Each thread a story, gently sewn,
Unraveling mysteries yet unknown.

Through mist and magic, we wander far,
Guided by the light of a distant star.
What secrets wait beyond the gate,
In realms where time sings soft and late?

Yet caution treads on fragile ground,
In silken hues, all truths surround.
For every wish may hold a price,
In this dance of fate, be wise and nice.

So weave your dreams with tender care,
Through the veil, take heed, beware.
For in the depths of what we seek,
Lies magic's kiss on hearts so meek.

Tapestries of Oaths in Nature's Fold

In nature's fold where oaths are spun,
Threads of promise, two become one.
Leaves whisper secrets to the trees,
Binding hearts with ancient decrees.

With each dawn's light, the pledge renews,
A tapestry rich in vibrant hues.
Through trials faced and joys embraced,
In every moment, love is traced.

Rivers flow with stories shared,
In nature's bosom, spirits bared.
Mountains stand as solemn guards,
Witnessing dreams, fulfilling shards.

The winds carry vows on gentle sighs,
As blossoms bloom and softly rise.
Together in this sacred space,
Nature cradles their gentle grace.

So honor the bonds, let them unfold,
In every leaf, let love be bold.
For in this world of fleeting time,
Tapestries of oaths forever rhyme.

Chasing Fables Across Sylvan Canvases

In the glade where whispers weave,
Tales of old begin to breathe.
With each step, the leaves confide,
Secrets in the moonlight hide.

Painted dreams on bark and stone,
Echoes of a magic grown.
Fairies flit and shadows play,
In the dawning of the day.

Winding paths of silver mist,
Every moment, a new twist.
With the stars, our hearts entwine,
Chasing fables, bright as wine.

Mossy boughs and laughter's sound,
Sylvan stories all around.
With each breath, adventure's light,
Guides us through the tranquil night.

In the forest, time stands still,
Fables woven at will.
Chasing echoes, hand in hand,
Across this enchanted land.

Threads of the Starlit Weaver

Underneath the cosmic glow,
Where the wispy breezes flow.
Starlit threads in dark embrace,
Weaving dreams in endless space.

From the loom of night so deep,
Tales of wonder start to creep.
Galaxies in silver dance,
Echoes of a fateful chance.

Every twinkle holds a story,
Glistening in ethereal glory.
Spinning worlds with gentle care,
Softly waking hearts laid bare.

Whispers beckon from afar,
Guiding wishes like a star.
Threads of fate, a binding song,
Binding us where we belong.

In the tapestry's embrace,
Fate and freedom find their place.
Underneath this wondrous sky,
With the stars, we learn to fly.

Sketched Shadows of Elfin Whimsy

In the woods where shadows sway,
Elfin laughter leads the way.
With a flicker, a playful jest,
Magic lingers, never rest.

Petals dance in soft twilight,
Chasing sparkles in the night.
Every footprint leaves a mark,
Whimsy glows within the dark.

Drawing secrets on the breeze,
Fleeting moments, hearts at ease.
With a sigh, they flutter near,
Elfin whispers, sweet and clear.

Cascading down the ancient tree,
The shadows hum, wild and free.
Sketching dreams on nature's page,
Fables whispered, age to age.

In the twilight, dance and spin,
With a laugh, the tales begin.
Through the forest, hand in hand,
Elfin whimsy at our command.

Lullabies of the Woodland Spirit

Cradled in the midnight air,
Softly sung with tender care.
Nature's heart, a gentle guide,
Whispering where dreams reside.

Rustling leaves hum sweet refrain,
Calling forth the magic's gain.
In the hush, the woodland sleeps,
Cradled tight in secrets deep.

Moonlight glows on mossy beds,
While the night sky gently spreads.
Lullabies in every sigh,
Wrapped in twilight's softest tie.

With each note, the echoes swell,
Casting long, enchanting spells.
In the arms of shadows bright,
Woodland spirits take their flight.

Through the night, their voices flow,
Guiding dreams where wild things grow.
In this space of endless grace,
Lullabies weave time and place.

Timeless Threads in a Whispering Grove

In the grove where shadows play,
Whispers echo night and day.
Ancient trees with secrets old,
Guard the tales yet to be told.

Moonlight dances on the stream,
Casting silver on a dream.
Branches sway in gentle breeze,
Carrying thoughts with such ease.

A bridge of stars above us glows,
Where every heart's desire flows.
Nature's breath, a soft embrace,
Weaving time in this sacred space.

Footprints left by souls long gone,
In this place, we all belong.
Each rustling leaf, a memory,
Of life's rich tapestry.

Here amidst the fading light,
Hope ignites the coming night.
The grove's embrace, a warm cocoon,
Where dreams awaken, softly bloom.

Gentle Reveries of the Enchanted Glade

In the glade where fairies dance,
Amidst the flowers, lost in trance.
Golden rays of sunbeam's glow,
Whisper soft, the secrets flow.

Mossy stones, a place to rest,
Nature's cradle, truly blessed.
Butterflies in colors bright,
Weave a tapestry of light.

Laughter echoes through the air,
Carried forth without a care.
A melody the trees replay,
As time softly slips away.

With every petal's gentle fall,
The heart remembers, after all.
In this realm, where dreams take flight,
Shadows chase the fading light.

From dusk to dawn, the magic sings,
Crickets chirp, and evening brings.
A tranquil night, beneath the moon,
Within this glade, we find our tune.

The Hidden Currents of the Sylvan World

In the woods where secrets lie,
Nature's map beneath the sky.
Silent streams that weave and flow,
Tell the tales we yearn to know.

Ancient stones, a watchful gaze,
Witness to the shifting days.
Roots entwined beneath the earth,
Hold the whispers of their worth.

Every rustle bears a sign,
Of life's tale, a grand design.
In the shade of leafy green,
Magic hums, though rarely seen.

From the ground to heaven's height,
Bridges formed in pure starlight.
The heart connects to all that breathes,
In the dance of autumn leaves.

Within the air, a spark ignites,
Guiding souls through endless nights.
The forest knows the paths we tread,
Carved in echoes, life is led.

Pathways on the Verge of the Unseen

Along the path where shadows merge,
A whispered call begins to surge.
Footsteps taken, soft and slow,
Curious hearts in overgrown.

Moonlit glimmers spark the dark,
Each step a thread, each breath a spark.
Hidden realms await our quest,
In the night, we find our rest.

The world around us starts to fade,
As dreams unspool, gently laid.
Voices call from far away,
Guiding us through night to day.

With every turn, a glimpse of grace,
Revealing wonders, our true place.
In this realm, both old and new,
The unseen beckons, calling true.

Paths diverge, yet still we roam,
Woven together, we find home.
Here on the edge, may we believe,
In the magic we receive.

Pillars of Silence beneath the Elder Trees

In twilight's glow, they stand so tall,
Guardians of whispers, heed their call.
Beneath boughs woven in ancient tales,
Echoes linger where the stillness prevails.

Their shadows cradle a timeless space,
Where secrets rest, and dreams embrace.
Breath of the forest, soft and deep,
Among their roots, the stillness creeps.

Each leaf a story, each branch a prayer,
In solemn grace, they weave the air.
Elder trees, keepers of the night,
In your silence, the world feels right.

Moonlight dances on mossy ground,
While owls in wisdom, silently abound.
A vigil held 'neath starlit skies,
In reverence, nature softly sighs.

These pillars rise as time moves on,
A testament to the whispered song.
In their embrace, all fears will cease,
Pillars of silence, grant us peace.

The Collected Sighs of Expectant Flora

In every bud, a secret breath,
Softly murmurs life and death.
Cradled in petals, hope unfolds,
The collected sighs of tales untold.

Dew-kissed mornings, bright and meek,
Whisper promises that nature seeks.
Gentle stirrings, the earth's delight,
Flora's musings, hidden from sight.

Each bloom unfurls, a prelude sweet,
To the dance of life, a rhythmic beat.
Amidst the green, where shadows dwell,
Their breath released, a soothing spell.

In sunlight's hand, they stretch and sway,
Embracing warmth, they find their way.
A chorus rises as petals gleam,
The collected sighs form a dream.

Time whispers softly through rustling leaves,
In every heart, a truth perceives.
Nature's pulse, a sacred lore,
Awake, expectant, forevermore.

A Symphony of Shadows in the Thicket

As twilight comes, the shadows play,
In thickets dense, where night meets day.
Whispers weave through branches tight,
A symphony unfolds in fading light.

Chords of silence stir the air,
Echoed notes of a world laid bare.
Creatures hidden beneath the brush,
In harmony, they move and hush.

The moon, a candle, dabs the night,
Painting shadows in gentle light.
Rustling leaves compose a tune,
A serenade beneath the moon.

Woodland creatures join in with glee,
In perfect time with ancient trees.
A symphony both wild and free,
In the thicket, they long to be.

With each passing hour, the echoes swell,
In rhythmic pulses, cast their spell.
A tapestry woven from dark and bright,
A symphony of shadows takes flight.

Hushed Revelations Among the Twisted Roots

Beneath the earth, where secrets twine,
Twisted roots in stories align.
Hushed revelations cradle the ground,
In silence fierce, the truths are found.

Veins of nature, intricately laced,
In every knot, a tale embraced.
Whispers born where shadows creep,
In twilight's grip, their secrets keep.

The mossy cloak, a soft disguise,
Where wonders lurk and magic lies.
Among the roots, deep and wise,
Hushed revelations softly rise.

Through tangled paths and undergrowth,
The tales converge, a shared oath.
Promises whispered in the dark,
Alight the mind, ignite a spark.

In nature's cradle, all is sent,
A world of wisdom, pure and bent.
Among the twisted roots, we see,
Hushed revelations set us free.

The Silence of Sighs in the Underwood

In the heart of the whispering wood,
Where shadows stretch and dreams once stood,
A sigh escapes on the breeze so light,
Carrying whispers into the night.

Beneath the boughs of the ancient trees,
Soft secrets dance on the murmuring leaves,
A tale of love in the cool twilight,
Where echoes linger, veiled from sight.

Moonbeams flicker like starlight's kiss,
Warming the coolness, crafting bliss,
Each rustle tells of a story rare,
Bound in the silence of twilight air.

Footsteps follow in delicate grace,
Lost in the dreams of this sacred space,
Where hearts entwine with each gentle sigh,
Underwood's magic, soaring high.

Yet still the night holds its breath so dear,
In the enchanted wood, all things sincere,
The silence hums, a melody sweet,
In the Underwood's arms, we find retreat.

Blossoms of Lore in Twilight's Caress

In twilight's embrace, soft petals unfold,
Tales of wonder and wisdom retold,
Blossoms of lore rise, kissed by the dew,
Each one a secret known only to few.

Golden glimmers through branches intertwined,
Life's fleeting moments, lovingly defined,
Swaying gently, where dreams come alive,
In this twilight realm, the heart will thrive.

A whisper of stories, both fragile and bright,
Painted in hues of the coming night,
Each blossom a memory, tender and true,
Fading like echoes when morning breaks through.

The essence of magic in twilight's soft shroud,
Each flower a promise, vibrant and proud,
Rooted in softness, they dance with the breeze,
A symphony sung with such effortless ease.

So cherish the moments the darkness does weave,
For in its soft cradle, we learn to believe,
Blossoms of lore whisper secrets of yore,
In twilight's caress, our spirits restore.

Cryptic Flight of Gossamer Spirits

On wings of silk, where the shadows play,
Gossamer spirits drift gently away,
In the twilight's shimmer, they seek their fate,
Whispering secrets, with time to create.

Through fields of light, on the wind they dance,
In a cryptic flight, like a fleeting glance,
Their laughter rings out in the cool, soft air,
Each shimmer a tale, beyond all compare.

Moonlit paths wind through the thicket deep,
Where echoes of magic in silence creep,
Chasing the dreams that the night does send,
In a tapestry woven, where shadows blend.

The night holds secrets of ancient lore,
In the gossamer flight that we all adore,
Each spirit a story that longs to be heard,
In the hush of the night, on the wings of a word.

So follow the trail where the spirits can lead,
In the depths of the night, we plant every seed,
With curious hearts, we will find our way,
In the cryptic flight of a star-kissed ray.

Tales Spun in the Misty Hours

When dawn's gentle fingers caress the sky,
Tales spun in the mist softly drift and sigh,
Veiled by the fog, wisdom finds its place,
In whispers of stories, in time's warm embrace.

The shadows unveil what the heart longs to know,
Through the shimmering veil, imaginations flow,
In the quiet of dawn, life's mysteries bloom,
Casting a glow in the soft morning gloom.

Each moment a thread in the fabric of dreams,
Woven with laughter, stitched close with seams,
The essence of time dances lightly and free,
As tales of the mist weave their tapestry.

Beneath the soft glow, the world starts to wake,
With echoes of memories, a delicate ache,
In the stories we hold, our hearts intertwine,
In the misty hours, our souls brightly shine.

So linger a while in the soft morning light,
As tales spun in mist take their destined flight,
Embrace the enchantment, let worries be few,
For in these still hours, the universe grew.

Sways of Spirit Among the Weaving Vines

In the quiet grace of twilight's glow,
Spirits dance where the wild vines grow.
Whispers echo through the tangled air,
Leaving traces of magic everywhere.

Moonlight weaves through leaves so bright,
Casting shadows in the soft twilight.
Every rustle holds a tale untold,
In a world where secrets unfold.

Glimmers of joy in the swaying branches,
With every sway, the soul enhances.
Lost in the embrace of nature's sigh,
Where dreams take flight and truly fly.

Came the wind, with playful tease,
Lifting spirits like autumn leaves.
Hearts entwined in this gentle place,
Finding solace in the vines' embrace.

So dance we will, 'neath the starlit skies,
Among the weaving vines, our spirits rise.
In this enchanted, ethereal domain,
We'll twine our laughter with the soft refrain.

Echoing Footfalls in the Dappled Wood

Footfalls sound on the forest floor,
Each step echoes through a hidden door.
Beneath the canopy, shadows play,
Guiding lost souls along the way.

Sunlight filters through leaves so green,
Illuminating spaces serene.
A rustle here, a whispered call,
In dappled wood, we hear it all.

With every twist of the winding path,
Life unveils its timeless math.
The ancient trees, with secrets vast,
Hold stories of both future and past.

Mysterious glades beckon us near,
Filling our hearts with unspoken cheer.
For in this haven, we come alive,
Where nature's soul helps us to thrive.

So let us wander, hand in hand,
In echoes of footfalls, we'll softly stand.
In the dappled wood, where magic flows,
Whispers of wonder in each breeze blows.

Frayed Edges of Memory Caught in the Wind

Frayed edges flutter, tattered and torn,
Memories linger, new ones are born.
Caught in the breeze, a wistful sigh,
In the dance of the past, we learn to fly.

Moments like fragments, scattered and bright,
Drifting through shadows, touched by the light.
In each gentle gust, we find our place,
Revisiting dreams in time's sweet embrace.

The laughter of children, the warmth of a tear,
Echoing softly, forever near.
In the canvas of life, each stroke will bend,
Crafting the story that has no end.

Through the corridors of time and space,
We gather the pieces we dare to face.
Wrapped in the whispers that the wind has spun,
Each frayed edge a tale, a life just begun.

So let us cherish the fluttering pages,
That tell of our lives through all of the ages.
For in the wind's embrace, we shall find,
The beauty of memory, intertwined.

Patterns of Existence Underneath the Pines

Beneath the pines, where silence reigns,
Nature pens its soft refrains.
A tapestry woven, a sacred art,
In patterns of life, every thread a part.

The needles whisper secrets in the breeze,
With every rustle, the spirit sees.
Dancing shadows on the forest floor,
Invite us to ponder what came before.

A squirrel dances, a leaf takes flight,
Patterns of existence, a wondrous sight.
Each heartbeat echoes in this sacred space,
Life blooms fiercely, yet wrapped in grace.

In the twilight, the world seems to still,
Reflecting the dreams that time can't kill.
For underneath the pines, we find our tune,
Singing with the stars beneath the moon.

So let us tread softly, in reverence and awe,
For patterns of existence hold nature's law.
In this hallowed ground, let our spirits climb,
Finding solace in every breath, every rhyme.

Music of the Meadow at Day's End

The sun dips low, a golden hue,
Whispers dance in twilight's view.
Crickets start their evening's song,
As shadows stretch and night grows long.

Butterflies flutter, soft and light,
Gathering dreams from day to night.
Gentle breezes through the grass,
In this moment, time will pass.

Stars begin to prick the sky,
As fading clouds in colors lie.
A symphony of scents so sweet,
Makes the melody complete.

The moon ascends, a silver glow,
Casting magic on the flow.
The meadow hums in soft refrain,
Where peace and wonder shall remain.

Here in whispers, hearts will blend,
In music's arms, we find a friend.
A serenade of nature's tune,
In love with dusk, beneath the moon.

The Curious Art of Nature's Palette

Brush strokes wide, the forest's art,
In colors bright, they play their part.
Emerald leaves, like jewels, shine,
In nature's frame, a world divine.

Sketches hidden in the bark,
Whispers of stories, light and dark.
Crimson petals, saffron skies,
In every corner, beauty lies.

Rivers splash in hues so rare,
Mirroring the world's great flair.
A canvas stretched from hill to brook,
Inviting all to stop and look.

Misty mornings, soft and clear,
In every drop, a dream, a tear.
Nature paints with every breath,
A dance of life, embracing death.

So take a step in this grand show,
Let colors flow, let wonder grow.
The art of nature, wild and free,
Is but a glimpse of what can be.

Flickering Glimmers Among the Boughs

Fireflies sparkle in the night,
Dancing stars without the height.
Through the trees, they weave and roam,
Making the darkness feel like home.

Moonbeams stitch a silver thread,
Across the branches overhead.
In this realm of shadowed light,
Magic whispers, hearts take flight.

Glimmers soft beyond the glade,
In the hush, sweet dreams are made.
Rustling leaves tell tales untold,
As night reveals its wonders bold.

Crickets chirp a calming tune,
Beneath a watchful, caring moon.
Each flicker holds a fleeting wish,
Nature's kindness in every swish.

So linger here, let time suspend,
As starlit visions softly blend.
In flickering glimmers found anew,
The night reveals its magic true.

Camouflaged Reveries in Mossy Depths

Mossy blankets cloak the ground,
In shadows deep, where dreams abound.
Hidden creatures shift and sway,
In this enchanted, wild ballet.

Fern fronds curl, like whispers shy,
As nature's secrets float and lie.
Tales of twilight softly weave,
Among the roots where none perceive.

With every rustle, stories tease,
The murmurs of the ancient trees.
In tangled greenery they rest,
Where every heart can feel its best.

Textures blend in shades of green,
A world alive, yet seldom seen.
Camouflaged, the magic flows,
In these depths, the spirit knows.

So wander through this mystical space,
And let the tranquil peace embrace.
In reveries, both sweet and deep,
The mossy depths will guard your sleep.

Beneath the Borrowed Shade

In whispers soft, the branches sway,
A refuge sought from light of day.
Beneath the leaves, where shadows play,
Dreams unfurl in fleeting gray.

The gentle breeze, a tender sigh,
Tales of old that seem to fly.
In echoes lost, the moments die,
Yet here, my heart will learn to lie.

With creatures small that dance and dart,
This borrowed shade, it steals my heart.
A world apart, where lost can start,
In nature's arms, we find our part.

The sunlight streams in golden beams,
Caressing faces, hiding dreams.
And laughter mingles with soft screams,
As friendship blooms like whispered themes.

So here I dwell, in quiet grace,
Embraced by earth's warm, sweet embrace.
Beneath the borrowed shade, I face,
The magic found in every space.

The Fading Echo of Lantern Lights

When lanterns fade in dusky hours,
Their whispers fade like wilted flowers.
In twilight's grasp, the stillness towers,
As shadows weave through midnight powers.

The echoes linger, soft and low,
A tapestry of dreams in tow.
Where wishes flown like whispers flow,
In gentle arms, the secrets grow.

Each flicker holds a tale of old,
Of hearts entwined, and glances bold.
In silken night, our stories unfold,
In lantern light, the warmth consoled.

Yet as the stars begin to blink,
We gather 'round, the moments sink.
In candle's glow, we pause and think,
Of paths we walked, of love's sweet link.

So let us stand, as shadows seep,
Embraced by night, our dreams to keep.
In fading lights where memories leap,
A sacred bond, forever deep.

Starlit Patterns on Dew-Kissed Petals

The dawn awakes with gentle hues,
Upon the grass, where dreams infuse.
Dew-kissed petals in morning's muse,
Reflecting starlight, softly bruise.

Each blossom shines, a fleeting thought,
In fragrant lanes where time is caught.
The whispered tales of battles fought,
In every bloom, a lesson taught.

With starlit patterns, stories weave,
In nature's dance, we learn to believe.
Where every glance, a spell retrieves,
In colored strokes, the heart perceives.

Beneath the sky, where shadows blend,
In each petal's fold, a longing penned.
The night shall come, and dreams descend,
Yet here, in beauty, we still mend.

So wander forth on paths anew,
Where starlit whispers call to you.
In every hue, the world imbues,
A promise kept, a heart so true.

Celestial Patterns in a Sylvan Embrace

In sylvan depths, where magic thrums,
The stars descend with whispered drums.
In leafy arms, the heart succumbs,
To cosmic tales that softly hums.

Amidst the trees, where shadows play,
The moonbeams dance, in bright array.
With every step, old legends say,
Celestial patterns found their way.

The nightingale sings twilit songs,
Of wanderers where the heart belongs.
Each note a thread, where love prolongs,
In nature's choir, we all are strong.

With fragrant blooms that scent the breeze,
In harmony, our spirits ease.
The world dissolves to gentle tease,
As dreams unfold beneath the trees.

So linger here, as stardust flows,
In sylvan magic, joy bestows.
With every heartbeat, nature knows,
In celestial patterns, love still grows.